TOMASZ TOMASZEWSKI

Your first 5K run

A complete beginner's guide from the couch to the first 5K run

First published by Your Life Habits 2019

Copyright © 2019 by Tomasz Tomaszewski

All rights reserved. No part of this publication may be reproduced, stored or transmitted in any form or by any means, electronic, mechanical, photocopying, recording, scanning, or otherwise without written permission from the publisher. It is illegal to copy this book, post it to a website, or distribute it by any other means without permission.

Tomasz Tomaszewski has no responsibility for the persistence or accuracy of URLs for external or third-party Internet Websites referred to in this publication and does not guarantee that any content on such Websites is, or will remain, accurate or appropriate.

First edition

This book was professionally typeset on Reedsy.
Find out more at reedsy.com

Contents

Your Free Gift	1
Introduction	2
On your mark!	2
About me	2
What more do you need?	3
Why Should you run?	5
If you want to be strong – run	5
Health Benefits of Running	6
Emotional benefits of running	7
Common mistakes during training and their solutions	9
Weather	9
Starting too fast	10
Overtraining	10
Hills	11
Arm Movements	11
Strides	11
Shoes	12
Hydration	12
Breathing	12
Basic Safety	13
Practical Tips	14
Warm up	14
Optimal pace for you	16
Proper breathing	17
How should you breathe while running?	17
Listen to your body: Beware of injuries	17

Cooling down	18
Stretches	19
The Good Runner's Lifestyle	21
Diet for runners: Hydration and Nutrition	21
How about hydration?	22
Staying motivated	23
Popular apps for runners	24
Get Set!	26
Run and walk intensive workout	26
Ultra run workout	28
Three days a week run and walk workout	30
Three days a week ultra run workout	32
From walker to runner 8-week workout for ultra beginners	33
Summary	36
What are you waiting for?	36
Answers to Common Questions	38
Thank you	40
About the Author	41
Also by Tomasz Tomaszewski	43

Your Free Gift

Thank you for purchasing the book "Your First 5K Run: A complete beginner's guide from the couch to the first 5K run".

As a thank you gift, please take these 5 powerful videos that accompany my book and will put you strongly on your feet to start running! Have fun!

All these videos are available for free on my website, just click the link below:
https://yourlifehabits.com/power-video/

https://yourlifehabits.com/power-video/

Introduction

On your mark!

Hi! Prospective runner. You can't get any luckier: having this book in your hands. While you may find lots of information about running in this book, the major aim is to help you start your journey to becoming a good runner, by getting you equipped with all needed for your first 5K race. If you don't only read but get challenged to do the practical recommendations in this book, in a matter of 7 weeks, you will find yourself ready to GO.

As a bonus, I prepared for you ready-to-download workouts accompanying this book, that you can get for free from my website yourlifehabits.com. You will find links in "Get Set!".

Are you ready? Get on the track: On your mark; get set; not so fast. Let's take a few moments to discuss why I am the right person to introduce you to this.

About me

I am Tomasz and this is my short story...

Although life didn't start very easy for me, today, I am proud of myself, because I have turned my situation around, and now, I am a very happy man, a friend to my kids and wife, and enjoy my family life.

I live a healthy and sporty life, with a fine physical and mental attitude. I partake in fitness exercises regularly, and pay close attention to the nutrients

I get from food. Because of that, and with my high level of motivation as a plus, each year, I beat my own record for 10K run; the last one stands at 47 minutes 13 seconds.

This year my challenge is to run below 46 minutes. Are you feeling challenged yet? This is just the beginning.

Anyone would think life had always been easy for me.

I am very resourceful and I give my all in my place of work. I maintain a very good relationship with others and boost our team spirit. I thought it is just me, but every time I flash back to my past, I see I have not always been an amazing person, it must have been the sporty life, life of a good runner, that has changed everything about me for better.

Yes, running on the track is like life itself. You have to keep going and stay motivated. I was able to transfer my running lessons to my life experiences, and things definitely improved.

Earlier in life, I was not so optimistic. I struggled with every day issues: paying off a mortgage, loans, having an overwhelming job and a bully for a boss, growing small children and fixing their problems, having little time to/for myself.

Additional worries concerned my health; chronic stress and general feeling of decreasing physical condition.

Everything was too much for me, I felt overwhelmed and depressed.

I knew I had to change my life, so I changed my perspective, stopped worrying and started to actively forge my life. Mind you, step by step, I did it!

My mission and source of personal satisfaction is helping people by equipping them with information by sharing my knowledge, and experience for **everyone who wants to live happily and enjoy a well-balanced life with consensus to core values, self-esteem, beloved family, and a great job**.

What more do you need?

Now, let's get back to business:

The trick to starting a race, both in life and on track, are almost the same. Every race begins in the mind at the point where the racer finally convinces himself he has what it takes to **start.** Starting at the right time is a golden rule, and remaining focused regardless of the distraction is what a racer can never afford not to do.

Running however, is more than an exercise or a competition. To those who have found the secret, it is a very important part of their life because it has its way of affecting every part of you: The mental, physical, health, etc. The difference between a runner and a non-runner will always be obvious: whether they are found on or off the track.

The journey of a thousand miles, they say, begins with a single step. Although your dream in life may be to be able to run as far and as fast as possible, the first rule is STARTing; the best way to begin is the 5K; and the right time to begin is NOW!

This book is a practical guide on how you can have a fast transition from the slow, unmotivated you, to finding yourself ready for your first 5K race. It has some great nuggets that will keep you going for long, and although it is to help as a beginner, its sole aim is to make you start right, so that soon, you can be an amazing runner.

There are many benefits you stand to enjoy from running. You probably only know that it strengthens your muscles. But, there are more, which you will find below.

So, take your time to read every part of this book, and be ready to put whatever you read into practice. Develop a new habit towards running, encourage yourself (because no one will do it for you), inform your family and friends about your decision so they can help, and assist you attaining your goal (you have a standing 7-week goal in this manual).

Soon, you will find yourself in the presence of everyone; friends and family, cheering you on, and you will see how satisfactory it is to make your people proud, and more particularly, yourself.

If there are any words for you at this time, it is: "**KEEP READING!**"

Why Should you run?

If you want to be strong – run

An anonymous Greek carved some witty words on a wall. Although it's been long, the words remain golden:

"If you want to be strong – run; you want to be wise – run; you want to be beautiful - run."

Now, I will show how true that is.

"If you want to be strong – run."

Running regularly strengthens your muscular system and the postural muscles that are responsible for our posture and figure. It doesn't stop there. Running improves body locomotion, perfectly develops the physical fitness of the body by helping make circulatory and respiratory functions easy.

After improving the speed and coordination of the body, it also builds character strength by developing features like patience, resoluteness, and stubbornness in goal pursuit, endurance, systematic and resilience to adversity; as well as self-confidence and an eye for success.

"You want to be wise – run."

Changes in the chemical composition of the brain (increased levels of serotonin and endorphins - *the so-called hormones of happiness*), induced by physical effort, can prevent some forms of neuromuscular disorders (e.g. depression) and have a positive effect on our well-being. In addition, the moment of relaxation in the form of jogging at dawn or at dusk, in the park, or along the river, is a great way to unload emotions and preserve the "sober" and "fresh" mind.

"You want to be beautiful – run."

"Systematic training in the form of running prevents the aging process. It improves blood supply to the skin, which is better nourished and cleansed, thus; making you appearance more attractive. It helps to maintain or reduce body mass, to shape muscles (especially calves, thighs, and buttocks) and to build an athletic figure full of energy and vitality."

One thing is certain: the difference between a runner and someone who isn't would always be obvious. Even from the appearance and also the way of life. While there are many benefits of running, to make space for practical details, I will only inform you about a few health and emotional benefits.

Read on, and you will find you've got nothing to lose by being a runner.

Health Benefits of Running

Improves knee health

I understand that sometimes in life, someone must have convinced you that running won't help your knees. That's a wrong belief. It is proven that running will make them better. Not only your knees, it is proven that running gives strength to all other joints and bones in the body.

Running increases bone mass, and also helps in preventing any bone-loss that is age related. Running puts pressure on your knees, ankles, hips, and cartilages. It leads to continuous compression and expansion that strengthens the bones, cartilages and ligaments over time.

Gives better sleep

Start running and you can say good bye to the day of taking sedatives in order to have a sound sleep. After getting your body warm, feeling almost totally tired, stretching your muscles and other parts of the body after a long run, you drop on your bed, sleep comes easily because the whole body has been exercised and it would jump at the chance to rest before anything else.

Improves cardiovascular health

With running, your health gets stronger. Findings have shown that people who find time to run or jog for about 10 minutes each day have lower risks of death due to heart disease.

Burns calories

One of the fastest ways to weight loss is consistent exercise. Running will help you burn calories, although the amount burned would be different from person to person, the biggest determinant being how fast each person completes a mile.

Improves stress resistance

The way running goes, you try to beat your record each time, develop your endurance level, keep going even when you are getting tired, seeing nothing except the finish line. That immediately transfers to other aspects of life, especially when you are stressed. First, a non-runner would get stressed before a runner when exposed to the same level of stress-creating situation, also, a runner would get out of stress before a non-runner. While learning to run, you automatically develop your resistance to stress.

Reduces chances of death

This is the overall result of the health advantages of running. With stronger muscles, stronger heart, resistance to stress, and other advantages, there are reduced chances of death.

You really want to be a runner!

Emotional benefits of running

Running does not only promise you benefits in health, it promises emotional benefits too. Many runners have realised this, and that is why they can't stop running, even when there are many discouragements. Whereas there are many, I will point some out in the next few lines.

Healthier brain

Since running is a cardiovascular exercise, it naturally pumps oxygen-rich blood in to your brain. When this is done, it results in long-term improvement in mental processes. It is simple: the more you run, the more you feed your brain.

Brightens the mood

Running has its way of helping the body create neurotransmitters like serotonin and dopamine. The deficiency of these chemicals causes some form of depression, which means running has a way of helping anxiety and depression, giving you a brighter mood.

Better self esteem

Although this is not so scientifically proven, it has been noticed, and it is important to mention. Running keeps you fit, keeps you going, keeps you in good shape, and can increase confidence in yourself, which improves your self-esteem, and makes you trust in your abilities. It affects a variety of aspects of your life: confidence when you are around peers in school, at the office, or even when on vacation. Body-shaming is an abuse but try not to be a victim.

Improves feeling

Ever heard of *runner's high*? Running causes an increases in the body's natural production of endorphins, which can reduce pain and stress. When endorphins flood the brain due to intense running, you witness runner's high.

Stronger memory

Some studies have revealed continuous exercise can cause some positive changes to your hippocampus. The changes can improve how easily you learn things, as well as retention. It can reduce neurodegeneration, depression, and dementia in the elderly. Generally, running slows down the pace of cell degeneration.

All right! I understand you have seen the numerous advantages, and you can't wait to start running. However, this is a complete guide, and not just some common hint, so I will take you through everything step-by-step, so you can begin your race.

It is important to open your eyes to the common mistakes most beginners make when they start running. Ensure you don't make any of these mistakes as they might affect your motivation and cause you to lose focus.

Common mistakes during training and their solutions

Your motivation to run could end even before it gets fully started if you miss some things.

There are many people who have decided to run but dropped out somewhere in-between because they were not getting things right. They are always the most difficult set of people to be motivated. It is easier to get someone to start, than to get a quitter to continue.

That is why in this manual, before giving you the go-ahead to hit the road, I will provide a summary of mistakes that are quite common, but you shouldn't make.

That would be the difference between someone who jumped in the road and someone who read through this guide. If you put everything in check, then there is nothing that can stop you, except YOU!

Follow this guide and try not to forget. But if you do, pick up your guide to remind you.

Weather

Running in cold weather is not the same as running in hot weather. There are special considerations for both climates you should consider. Failure to take this into account, could have adverse effects and discourage you.

Running in cold weather requires wearing a thin layer of synthetic material such as polypropylene because it would wick sweat from your body. You should avoid cotton as that will retain moisture and keep you wet. If it is very cold, wear a bit thicker material but not a heavy layer that would weigh you down and keep you sweaty. Keep in mind, if you dress properly, you will stay warm. Also, if you run in the cold with snow, the glare from snow can result in snow blindness, so you should wear sunglasses. Wearing a pair of gloves isn't a bad idea either.

Running in hot weather requires "obeying your thirst," therefore, you need to find a way to stay hydrated. You should go for light-colored, loose-fitting clothing in this case. During hot season, you should either run early, or late. Try as much as possible to avoid running between 10:00am and 04:00pm.

Starting too fast

Many runners are quite eager at the beginning. They go as fast as they feel they can go but that is a wrong move if you are going for long distance. You must plan to run your last lap faster than your first, and the best way to do it is reserving energy and going a little slower at first.

Overtraining

Some runners feel they have to hit the road every time and not listen to their body. Yes, you must learn how to endure and beat your limit, but at the same time, you must learn how to give your muscles enough time to recover. This is the main cause of injury and burn out for runners. If you do not take this into account, you will end up losing all motivation to run. Your rest days are as important as your practice schedule. Never come out on your rest day to run. Also, find time for cross-training. Don't only run. Integrate other exercises in your physical activity.

Hills

There is a point in your training where you have to descend a hill. It is always fun to lean forward and give out control but it will do you no good. Whatever surface a runner finds him/ herself on, to avoid injury, and to make training pleasant, the runner must have full control of his/ her movement. Never give it away!

Arm Movements

Many beginners swing their arms side-to-side and that could interrupt the way you breathe. If you hold your hands too high towards your chest, it will get you tired quicker. To run effectively, you should try keeping your hands at your waist level, and they should be about 90-degree angle, with your elbows beside you. Swing hands back and forth at the shoulder, and not the elbow. Make sure your posture is straight, and when you are getting tired, press your chest out.

Strides

Beginners often believe that having longer strides increases their speed. That is wrong! You can get injured when you over-stride or land first on your heel with your leg far away in front of you. Not only that, it also wastes energy. Always try to land having your foot directly under your body, with your mid-sole. It is difficult to keep this, especially when running downhill. To keep your stride short and accurate, you have to keep your arm swings short and accurate. To get faster, don't over-stride, make your steps quick and light, as if the ground is burning your leg.

Shoes

You can get injured wearing too old or wrong type of running shoes. It is better to locate the nearest store to you that specializes in running equipment. There, you will find specialists who will check to know if you are an under-pronator, over-pronator, or a neutral runner. They can then make recommendations on the right shoe for you. After getting the right shoe, ensure you get new ones every 300-350 miles, if not, it could lead to loss of cushioning, and that could lead to injuries.

Hydration

Most beginners underestimate the amount of fluid they lose when running, so, they don't get accurately hydrated for the run to avoid side stiches, not knowing dehydration could affect both health and performance. As a runner, you must pay close attention to how much you drink during, before, and after running. It is important. One hour before you set out, you should drink 16-24 ounces of either water or any other non-caffeinated fluid. If you feel a bit thirsty again, take another 4-8 ounces before starting. While running, let your thirst decide when you will rehydrate. It could be simply water, but on longer runs or exercises, you should consume a sports drink to replace important minerals. It is equally necessary to rehydrate after your run. You should keep rehydrating after your run if your urine is dark yellow; it is supposed to be lemonade colour. You have to keep it accurate! Don't drink too much, don't drink too little.

Breathing

Some beginners don't know the right way to breathe when running, they start too shallow, and it can result in side stitches. Don't breathe in only through your nose when running. You are burning lots of energy and your muscles need oxygen to keep going. Your nostrils are too small to supply that, therefore, breathe in through both mouth and nose. Also, you should try to take deep breathes rather than just shallow ones from your chest. Breathe from your diaphragm (belly) so you avoid side stitches. Breathe out through your mouth. As a beginner, run at a pace at which you can breathe fine. A great clue is taking a "talk test." You should be able to say some words without gasping for breath. If unable to talk, reduce the speed.

Basic Safety

Practicing takes a lot of running on the road, but many people forget basic safety. Things are a little complex here because you are preparing to become a track runner. You must keep the track rules, to get used to them; but if you are running on the road, you must be attentive as you are not the only user of the road. You can use ear pods but keep the volume at a level that will not obstruct you from hearing noises around you. Also, understand how and when to stop if you become tired, and find a safe place to stop.

Practical Tips

There are some activities that make up the whole running process that you must be careful enough to do and do the right way. They make running run smoothly, and make the running experience better. These activities, among others, include: warming up, stretching, running, proper breathing, cooling down. I will give you some practical tips to help you do them the right way. This is the part of the guide you cannot afford to pass by or forget when you step out to run.

Warm up

As it was noted earlier, it is very injurious to listen to your enthusiasm that you feel like running, you burst out your door, and take it violently down the street. That way, you are not exercising the body, you are making it suffer. Take pizza for example. It is very tasty, but if you feed it to a week-old baby, it wouldn't go over well. Running is exactly like that. While our muscles love exercise and they have great chance of development during it, you have to take it bit by bit, to get them hyperactive, and make them able to take whatever you give them.

If you hit the road without first warming up, you run a great risk of ripping a tendon, dislocating a joint or bone; pulling a muscle; or any other running related injury. When you give your body the warmup it requires, you slowly get it into action, bring up your heart rate, and find it easy to take up the run from there.

So, now that you know that warming up is a must, you must be wondering how to do it the right way. I recommend a few activities for a beginner:

1. **Walk**: Start with a simple three to five-minute walk. The goal is starting at a pace that is not too fast for your body. It is the right way for a beginner to prepare their body to run because you use all the muscles you need to run, and that sends a signal to the brain that it will soon be time to go.
2. **Jog**: After walking for a while, you can start jogging. Do five to six 100-meter jogs, and that is enough for transition from walking mode to running mode. This should not take you less than two minutes. When getting to 60 meters, accelerate a bit, and when you are on 100, start to decelerate. After every 100 meters, take a calm walk and shake out your legs for 90 seconds. You have to be careful when jogging to ensure you are not over-striding. You have learnt about that before.
3. **Stretch**: Do some stretching for a while. I discourage static stretching where you hold a muscle in a position for seconds because it has been found to cause injury. The best kind is dynamic stretching that keeps all muscles strengthened. Do simple workouts that will engage your hands, legs, shoulders, elbows, and other parts you need to run. You can try skipping, squats, jumping jacks, jogging backwards, run on the spot with knees up to waist level, etc. Ensure you are not burning too much energy in whatever stretch you choose, so that you won't call it a day when it's time to run.

Now that you know the right way to warm up, it's time to learn running. Running is not as simple as swinging arms and picking up your legs, however, it is not difficult. If you get it right, it becomes one of the easiest things for you, and one major part of getting it right is running at the right pace. How do you know the right pace? I won't let it go unanswered!

Optimal pace for you

When talking about pace, the goal is to start well, get better, and then, be at your best. Don't forget, your best could be someone else's better, and your better could be someone else's best. There is always a difference in runners' base pace.

During training, the plan is always to give 60-70 percent, so that during the real run, you can give 100% and sometimes, 110%. As a runner, it is important for you to know your base pace. It will help you to know if you are giving below what you can give, or if you are too fast, going beyond what your body can afford. Although it is true beating the limit is a goal, it has to be step by step, and not a one-day breakthrough.

So, how do you find your base pace?

Start at a mile run at a steady, conversational pace. When done, go on second half mile at a pace you can only talk in short phrases. The pace you sustain in the second part is your base pace. Don't write it down yet, you will have to verify it a few days later.

After a few days, go on another one-mile run at your assumed base pace. In-between every 200 meters, jog 100 meters. If your third running stretch is as fast as the first one, then that is your baseline pace, but if you got slower with each run, calculate an average of the three runs, and that can be recorded as your baseline pace. You can try to improve on the pace through training, however, be careful not to overdo it.

You can also get some help using a pace calculator, which would help you decide how fast you must be to finish a run at a particular time; help you calculate your pace; also help you calculate your distance.

You can find any of them at a local athletics store, and you can find some online calculators like this.

That known, it is important to understand proper breathing when running.

Proper breathing

Breathing the right way is as important in running as every other thing. If done wrong, you may gas out easily, get side stiches, or sometimes, end up on the floor and take minutes before recovering.

How should you breathe while running?

There is no much instruction here, you only have to consciously take a deep breath, and not the shallow one. It is called breathing at the stomach level. Breathing at the chest level may be easy and fast, but you run the risk of getting tired easily, as well as having side stitches. When you breathe at the stomach level, you get enough air for every part of your lungs and avoid side stiches.

You can start practicing stomach-level breathing off the road. Lie on a sofa facing up, put a book or any other light object on your stomach, then, start breathing. If you are breathing at the stomach level, you are supposed to see the book, obviously, going up and coming down. Keep doing it until you master how to do it.

It is important to breathe through both mouth and nose, and not the nose only. Come on, you are going on an energy sapping activity, your small nostrils cannot give your body all the oxygen it needs. Help it with your mouth. I often advise while learning to breathe the stomach level, you should also learn how to do it using mouth and nose. If you get it right, you will find you have better energy to complete races, and you will feel better running.

Now, you might get everything right some times, but the body is not in the mood to go. You don't have a choice; you must listen to your body. What does that mean?

Listen to your body: Beware of injuries

If you are a runner and you don't have minor injuries, then, there is almost every certainty that you are not giving your all. This does not mean injuries are necessary identity for runners, however, you almost cannot avoid thigh or arm pains. What should you do when you feel that?

Listening to your body is very important. When you feel such pains, many people think going on in pain will make them better. No! That's a lie! When you are training in pains, you are most likely underperforming, and there is no development in that. When you train to the extent your body starts showing vital signs, take a break! Yes, the goal is going a bit beyond your limit, it is not tearing your muscle or other tissues.

Many beginners are always scared if they give up easily the first time and next time, it is possible they get entirely lay and stop observing their training schedules. You are the only one who can help yourself out! Be disciplined! Take your schedule serious, but your body more seriously.

Most minor injuries can heal during simple and cross trainings. For example, you felt pains when running up the road, you don't necessarily have to quit running to heal. You can run slower on a flat terrain where you won't be stressing your muscles beyond what it can take. If you are feeling slight pains in your shoulders, you can try training that does not require too much use of hands.

Most runners who refuse to listen to their bodies end up nursing bigger injuries than when the symptoms came. Those who listen to their bodies recover quickly, come back stronger, and give their best. You definitely want to join the latter group!

Cooling down

Just as you start your race by warming up, you have to end it by cooling down. While warming sends a signal to the body that it is time for race, cooling down tells you it is time to rest. Having beat your limit during training, cooling down helps muscles recover to their original state. While warming up, you get heartrate increased, cooling down, you gradually bring it back to its normal state. How should you do this?

Most times, a five to ten-minute slow walk is enough, but if you want to add more, you can take some dynamic stretches. You can choose to do it a different way by taking off your shoes and walking barefoot on the grass. If you feel walking is too slow for you, you can go a little faster, into a very slow jogging exercise. Cooling down keeps you strong and ready for the next training, and it aids recovery a lot. for the next training

Stretches

Although I often discourage too much static stretches after an intense training session so that you don't put too much pressure on a particular muscle, there are ways to do it right, and it can't be other than spending just a few seconds before changing the part concentrated on.

The following are simple static stretches you can try after your training and the seconds you have to hold for. They shouldn't give you pain. If you do feel pain while trying them, quit immediately!

1. **Thigh Stretch (15 seconds)**: Grab the front of your right foot with your right hand, then, move your heel towards your buttocks. You can place your hand on a wall or any other thing for balance. Repeat for the left leg.
2. **Hamstring Stretch (15 seconds)**: Stand straight, then, put your right leg in front of the left one making the toes face up, grab your waist, then, bend you left leg. Repeat for the other leg.
3. **Calf Stretch (15 seconds)**: With both legs facing forward, move your right leg to the front, then, bend towards the leg at the front while holding your hips. Make sure the leg at the back is straight. Repeat it for the other leg.
4. **Buttock Stretch (15 seconds)**: Lie on your back with your knees bent. Make sure both feet are touching the floor, then, cross your right leg over your left thigh, grab the back of the left thigh with both hands, and lift it towards your chest. If you can't hold for 15 seconds, drop it immediately, then, repeat the same routine for the other leg.
5. **Lower Back Stretch (15 seconds)**: Lie on your back with your legs stretched out on the floor. Lift your left knee towards your chest and hold for 15 seconds. Repeat it for the second leg also, then hold both knees towards your chest.

These are all practical tips to successfully completing activities related to running in the easiest and safest way.

Now, let's go deep into more on a runner's lifestyle. You can't afford to miss the next section.

The Good Runner's Lifestyle

Diet for runners: Hydration and Nutrition

As a runner, you don't only need to keep your diet balanced for good health, but because it has a say in how well you perform. Being on the right diet can aid performance and that is what a beginner should aim for.

For a runner, the right diet will have enough proportion of carbohydrates, protein, fats, vitamins, and minerals.

Let's see why they are all important and what they will offer you.

- **Carbohydrates**: Of your total calorie intake as a runner, carbohydrates should make up 60%. It is proven they are the best source of energy for athletes. You might get a little from proteins and fats, but energy from carbs are very efficient. Foods like potatoes, whole grain breads, rice, whole grain pasta, starchy vegetables, fruits, are all highly encouraged for runners.
- **Protein**: Although protein also gives energy, their most contribution to the runner's body is the repair of tissues damaged while training. When trying weight loss and want to reduce your food intake, proteins keep you fuller for longer. It should make up 15% of a runner's daily intake. Go for sources of protein that are low in cholesterol and fat like lean meats, low-fat dairy products, beans, fish, whole grains, poultry, etc.
- **Fat**: A diet high in fats can cause more harm than good to the runner, therefore, ensure your daily intake is never more than 20%. Go for foods

that are low in cholesterol and saturated fats. You need about 3,000 mg of omega-3 fat a day because omega-3 prevents some diseases, and is vital for good health. Foods like oils, nuts, and cold-water fish will give you enough of that.
- **Vitamins**: It is true that vitamins may not give you energy, but they are still very important. During exercise, compounds named free radicals may be produced, and they are very dangerous to cells. Vitamins A, C, and E work as great antioxidants to neutralize the effects of the free radicals. However, you are advised to get your vitamins from whole foods and not supplements because supplements are not proven to improve health or performance.
- **Minerals**: Minerals like Calcium, Iron, Sodium and other electrolytes must feature in a runner's diet. Calcium will protect against osteoporosis and stress fractures. You can get calcium from eggs, vegetables, calcium-fortified juices, low-fat dairy products. Iron will deliver oxygen to your cells so you don't experience fatigue easily. You can get them from lean meats, scallops, nuts, and shrimp. When you sweat during exercise, you lose sodium and other electrolytes. If you take a balanced diet, they are naturally replaced, but there are times you find yourself craving salty foods. It can be your body's gentle way of informing you to get sodium. Go for sports drinks or eat some pretzels.

How about hydration?

As stated earlier in this guide, runners cannot afford to get dehydrated. Take water almost as fast and as much as your body demands. You should take sports drinks often as well. They are loaded with almost all nutrients you need, and can get, from a liquid substance.

Running does not stop you from eating anything, it only needs you to be conscious of the nutrient intake. So, dear runner, go ahead, have the tasty smoothie, fruits, yoghurt, chocolate milk, eat anything! But be sure you are taking the right proportion of nutrients, and steer away from cholesterol!

Staying motivated

Motivation is very important. If you get on the road as fast the urge develops in you but refuse to find a way to keep the fire burning, there is almost every chance that the schedule will seem too difficult for you to continue, and you will end up being a dropout runner. Motivation has to be deliberately found by the runner, and the following tips will help you:

- **Run with Friends:** You can join a running club, or talk a friend into going through your schedule with you. It is going to benefit both parties, definitely. When you run with a friend, there is a seemingly unannounced competition that starts. You don't want to get tired when your friend is still going, and you don't want to stay way back when the friend is far in front. Both runners will be on their toes.
- **Keep notes:** After each training, write something down about the distance covered and the time spent. Put an overall comment like, "Amazing, I felt strong," or "I got tired earlier than usual." Somehow, because you are conscious you are keeping a record, you will always want to do better than the last try. It will also help to set goals and meet them.
- **Choose a mantra:** Get a slogan that keeps you encouraged, and keeps you going. You keep playing it in your head, and can sometimes say it out loud when running. It could be something like, "My race My Pace" "Finish what you start" "Quitters are not winners!" "Easy does it!" "Never give up!" "Slow and steady wins the race!" "The faster, the better!"
- **Talk to runners:** If your motivation is not enough, look for runners and talk to them. They will tell you a lot of amazing things that will keep you going.
- **Reward yourself**: When you set goals and meet them, don't let it go unnoticed. Treat yourself like a winner. Buy yourself new clothing, get a great massage, do whatever makes you happy. It doesn't mean you have to spend money every time you are amazing, if there's an item of clothing you want to buy, you can decide to wait until you meet a goal before buying it. That keeps you going.

- **Don't say "all or nothing"**: Sometimes, because of a schedule, you don't have enough hours to train. Don't miss it because of that. Go out, even if it is just for 20 minutes. You will gain something from it, and it will help you avoid missing training every now and then.
- **Remind yourself of the health benefits:** Remind yourself there is nothing to lose as a runner. Tell yourself your shape will get better, your health state too. Train each time, remembering you are doing yourself some good.
- **Make your goals known:** When you tell people about your goals and the time to accomplish them, you don't want to look like a failure to them, so you pursue them with all your might. Paste your schedule at home, at work, everywhere. Then, state your goals too. You will be reminded by friends, and when you achieve them, you can have a friend join in your adventure.
- **Make it fun**: That's the biggest advice here. Don't let your schedule be like another kind of work you must do after leaving office. Make it fun. Don't say "no pain, no gain," say "no fun, no run."

Popular apps for runners

The following are useful apps for runners, especially beginners:

1. **COUCH TO 5K(C25K)**: Very good for beginners because it will help you through your training. This particular one is made for a prospective 5K runner, and that makes it one of the best options for you. It guides you through your workouts and keeps track of your stats and routes.
2. **STRAVA:** This helps you develop within a group and not alone. If you love a gentle competition, then, go on Strava and you will find many people waiting to compete with you. Yes, even beginners. You can create a group, set goals, and know who meets it and who doesn't. It is available on iOS, Android, and Apple Watch.
3. **RUNKEEPER:** One of the most popular and most effective running apps. It uses GPS to track your distance, time, and space. You can set goals

with it and watch your stats to remain motivated. It has reminders that prompt you so you can reach your training goals. It can sync with other running apps and devices like Fitbit, Apple watch, etc. It is available without any payment on iOS or Android.

4. **RUNSTATIC**: This is one of the best apps out there for both iOS and Andriod devices. It gives you training plans for different types of races. There is the option of saving your routes as well as your stats. It keeps you motivated, always trying to beat your record. You can post on social media after your run so your friends can see, and it syncs with some other apps like MyFitnessPal, Garmin devices, etc.

5. **ENDOMONDO**: It has lots of features, but it is making this list because of its great social features added to the running ones. It is a personal training app, you can set goals with it, analyze your stats, use GPS during your training, and also connect with millions of athletes all around the world who will keep you motivated.

Get Set!

Having learnt a lot about running and all it takes to start, it is the right time to show you what your training schedule will look like for the next seven weeks. You can put in some changes to suit your schedule and strength but try as much as possible to do all tasks and meet all durations.

There are five different training schedules for a beginner. Depending on your work schedule and the number of days you can spare in a week to train, you can choose from any of them. Depending on your strength, go for the first two if you want a seven days a week plan, or the second two if all you have to offer is three days a week.

If first four workouts seem to be too hard for you, I have a plan dedicated to ultra beginners. In this case you will need eight weeks to prepare yourself and on the ninth week you will be ready for your first 5K Run!

These plans involve running workouts per week. On the days you're not running, it's OK to work your muscles in other ways by doing different forms of cardio, strength-training sessions, or yoga or flexibility training. Listen to your body and adjust the schedule as needed to allow for much-needed recovery time. Begin each workout with a five-minute warmup, followed by a five-minute cooldown.

Run and walk intensive workout

For an added bonus, click this link and it will take you to my site where you can grab the 5K workout plan: http://yourlifehabits.com/books/your-first-5k-run/runwalk/

WEEK 1
    DAY 1 Run for 5 minutes; Walk for 1 minute; Repeat 5 times.
    DAY 2 Rest
    DAY 3 Run for 5 minutes; Walk for 1 minute; Repeat 5 times.
    DAY 4 Cross-train for 40-45 minutes.
    DAY 5 Rest
    DAY 6 Run for 6 minutes; Walk for 1 minute; Repeat 5 times.
    DAY 7 Rest or take a 30-minute walk.

WEEK 2
    DAY 1 Run for 7 minutes; Walk for 1 minute; Repeat 4 times.
    DAY 2 Rest
    DAY 3 Run for 7 minutes; Walk for 1 minute; Repeat 4 times.
    DAY 4 Cross-train for 40-45 Minutes.
    DAY 5 Rest
    DAY 6 Run for 8 minutes; Walk for 1 minute; Repeat 4 times.
    DAY 7 Rest or take a 30-minute walk.

WEEK 3
    DAY 1 Run for 9 minutes; Walk for 1 minute; Repeat 3 times.
    DAY 2 Rest
    DAY 3 Run for 9 minutes; Walk for 1 minute; Repeat 3 times.
    DAY 4 Cross-train for 45 minutes.
    DAY 5 Rest
    DAY 6 Run for 11 minutes; Walk for 1 minute; Repeat 3 times.
    DAY 7 Rest or take a 30-minute walk.

WEEK 4
    DAY 1 Run for 12 minutes; Walk for 1 minute; Repeat 3 times.
    DAY 2 Rest
    DAY 3 Run for 14 minutes; Walk for 1 minute; Repeat 3 times.
    DAY 4 Cross-train for 45 minutes.

DAY 5 Rest

DAY 6 Run for 15 minutes; Walk for 1 minute; Repeat 2 times.

DAY 7 Rest or take a 30-minute walk.

WEEK 5

DAY 1 Run for 16 minutes; Walk for 1 minute; Run for 12 minutes.

DAY 2 Rest

DAY 3 Run for 18 minutes; Walk for 1 minute; Run for 10 minutes.

DAY 4 Cross-train for 45 minutes.

DAY 5 Rest

DAY 6 Run for 20 minutes; Walk for 1 minute; Run for 10 minutes.

DAY 7 Rest or take a 30-minute walk.

WEEK 6

DAY 1 Run for 23 minutes; Walk for 1 minute; Run for 5 minutes.

DAY 2 Rest

DAY 3 Run for 24 minutes; Walk for 1 minute; Run for 5 minutes.

DAY 4 Cross-train for 45 minutes.

DAY 5 Rest

DAY 6 Run for 25 minutes; Walk for 1 minute; Run for 5 minutes.

DAY 7 Cross-train for 30 minutes.

WEEK 7

Start! Your First 5K

Now, that may be too easy and unchallenging for you (although being a beginner, I strongly doubt). You can try the next timetable.

Ultra run workout

For an added bonus, click this link and it will take you to my site where you can grab the 5K workout plan: http://yourlifehabits.com/books/your-first-5k-run/ultra-run-workout/

WEEK 1
- **DAY 1** Rest
- **DAY 2** Run 1 mile
- **DAY 3** Rest or Cross-train for 40 minutes
- **DAY 4** Run 1 mile
- **DAY 5** Rest
- **DAY 6** Run 1.5 miles
- **DAY 7** Run for 20 minutes or Cross-train

WEEK 2
- **DAY 1** Rest
- **DAY 2** Run 1.5 miles
- **DAY 3** Rest or Cross-train for 40 minutes
- **DAY 4** Run 1.5 miles
- **DAY 5** Rest
- **DAY 6** Run 1.75 miles
- **DAY 7** Run for 20 minutes or Cross-train

WEEK 3
- **DAY 1** Rest
- **DAY 2** Run 2 miles
- **DAY 3** Rest or Cross-train for 40 minutes
- **DAY 4** Run 1.5 miles
- **DAY 5** Rest
- **DAY 6** Run 2 miles
- **DAY 7** Run for 20 minutes or Cross-train

WEEK 4
- **DAY 1** Rest
- **DAY 2** Run 2.25 miles
- **DAY 3** Rest or Cross-train for 40 minutes
- **DAY 4** Run 1.5 miles
- **DAY 5** Rest

DAY 6 Run 2.25 miles
DAY 7 Run for 30 minutes or Cross-train

WEEK 5
DAY 1 Rest
DAY 2 Run 2.5 miles
DAY 3 Rest or Cross-train for 40 minutes
DAY 4 Run 2 miles
DAY 5 Rest
DAY 6 Run 2.5 miles
DAY 7 Run for 30 minutes or Cross-train

WEEK 6
DAY 1 Rest
DAY 2 Run 2.75 miles
DAY 3 Cross-train for 40 minutes
DAY 4 Run 2 miles
DAY 5 Rest
DAY 6 Run 2.75 miles
DAY 7 Run for 35 minutes or Cross-train

WEEK 7
Start! Your First 5K

If what you have to offer is just three days a week, then go for the following schedule.

Three days a week run and walk workout

For an added bonus, click this link and it will take you to my site where you can grab the 5K workout plan: http://yourlifehabits.com/books/three-days-a-week-run-and-walk-workout/

WEEK 1
DAY 1 5 × 1 minute running with an interval of 1 minute walk
DAY 2 6 × 1 minute running with an interval of 1 minute walk
DAY 3 4 × 2 minute running with an interval of 1 minute walk

WEEK 2
DAY 1 5 × 2 minute running with an interval of 1 minute walk
DAY 2 4 × 3 minute running with an interval of 1 minute walk
DAY 3 2 × 3 minute running with an interval of 1 minute walk + 2 minute walk + 2 × 5 minute run with a break of 2 minutes

WEEK 3
DAY 1 2 × 3 minute running with an interval of 1 minute walk + 2 minute walk + 2 × 5 minute run with a break of 1 minute
DAY 2 4 × 5 minute running with an interval of 1 minute walk
DAY 3 2 × 5 minute running with an interval of 1 minute walk + 2 minute walk + 2 × 6 minute run with a break of 2 minutes

WEEK 4
DAY 1 3 × 6 minute running with an interval of 1 minute walk
DAY 2 2 × 6 minute running with an interval of 1 minute walk + 2 minute walk + 10 minute run
DAY 3 2 × 8 minute running with an interval of 1 minute walk + 2 minute walk + 12 minute run

WEEK 5
DAY 1 2 × 12 minutes running with an interval of 1 minute walk
DAY 2 12 minutes running + 1 minute walk + 15 minutes run
DAY 3 15 minutes running + 1 minute walk + 20 minutes run

WEEK 6
DAY 1 25 minutes running
DAY 2 free time

DAY 3 25 minutes running

WEEK 7
   Start! Your First 5K

Again, that may be too easy and unchallenging for you (although being a beginner, I strongly doubt). You can try the following timetable.

Three days a week ultra run workout

For an added bonus, click this link and it will take you to my site where you can grab the 5K workout plan: http://yourlifehabits.com/books/three-days-a-week-ultra-run-workout/

WEEK 1
   DAY 1 5 minutes of run
   DAY 2 6 minutes of run
   DAY 3 8 minutes of run

WEEK 2
   DAY 1 10 minutes of run
   DAY 2 12 minutes of run
   DAY 3 15 minutes of run

WEEK 3
   DAY 1 15 minutes of run
   DAY 2 17 minutes of run
   DAY 3 20 minutes of run

WEEK 4
   DAY 1 15 minutes of run
   DAY 2 20 minutes of run
   DAY 3 25 minutes of run

WEEK 5
>**DAY 1** 20 minutes of run
>**DAY 2** 25 minutes of run
>**DAY 3** 30 minutes of run

WEEK 6
>**DAY 1** 25 minutes of run
>**DAY 2** free time
>**DAY 3** 25 minutes of run

WEEK 7
Start! Your First 5K

From walker to runner 8-week workout for ultra beginners

If you don't feel like a runner born overnight I have an ultra easy workout for you. Here's an eight-week plan that will get you running for 30 minutes which should equal to 5K distance. It takes weeks of building up and training the body to get used to moving this way. Whether you enjoy running outside in the fresh air, or hitting the treadmill at your gym, this plan will turn you into a runner in just two months.

This plan involves three running workouts per week. On the days you're not running, it's OK to work your muscles in other ways by doing different forms of cardio, strength-training sessions, or yoga or flexibility training. As always, listen to your body and adjust the schedule as needed to allow for much-needed recovery time. Begin each workout with a five-minute warmup, followed by a five-minute cooldown.

For an added bonus, click this link and it will take you to my site where you can grab the 5K workout plan: https://yourlifehabits.com/books/from-walker-to-runner-ultra-beginner-workout/

WEEK 1
   DAY 1 Walk for 2 minutes; Run for 1 minute; Repeat 7 times = 21 minutes.
   DAY2 Walk for 2 minutes; Run for 2 minute; Repeat 6 times = 24 minutes.
   DAY3 Walk for 2 minutes; Run for 3 minute; Repeat 5 times = 25 minutes.

WEEK 2
   DAY 1 Walk for 1 minutes; Run for 3 minute; Repeat 7 times = 28 minutes.
   DAY2 Walk for 1 minutes; Run for 4 minute; Repeat 5 times = 25 minutes.
   DAY3 Walk for 1 minutes; Run for 5 minute; Repeat 5 times = 30 minutes.

WEEK 3
   DAY 1 Walk for 1 minutes; Run for 6 minute; Repeat 4 times = 28 minutes.
   DAY2 Walk for 1 minutes; Run for 7 minute; Repeat 4 times = 32 minutes.
   DAY3 Walk for 1 minutes; Run for 8 minute; Repeat 4 times = 36 minutes.

WEEK 4
   DAY 1 Run for 8 minutes; Walk for 1 minute; Run for 9 minutes; Walk for 1 minute; Repeat 2 times = 38 minutes
   DAY 2 Run for 9 minutes; Walk for 1 minute; Run for 9 minutes; Walk for 1 minute; Repeat 2 times = 40 minutes
   DAY 3 Run for 9 minutes; Walk for 1 minute; Run for 10 minutes; Walk for 1 minute; Repeat 2 times = 42 minutes

WEEK 5
   DAY 1 Run for 10 minutes; Walk for 1 minute; Run for 10 minutes; Walk for 1 minute; Repeat 2 times = 42 minutes
   DAY 2 Run for 10 minutes; Walk for 1 minute; Run for 12 minutes = 23 minutes
   DAY 3 Run for 12 minutes; Walk for 1 minute; Run for 15 minutes = 28 minutes

WEEK 6
   DAY 1 Run for 15 minutes; Walk for 1 minute; Run for 15 minutes = 31 minutes

DAY 2 Run for 15 minutes; Walk for 1 minute; Run for 18 minutes = 34 minutes

DAY 3 Run for 18 minutes; Walk for 1 minute; Run for 20 minutes = 39 minutes

WEEK 7

DAY 1 Run for 10 minutes; Walk for 1 minute; Run for 21 minutes = 32 minutes

DAY 2 Run for 10 minutes; Walk for 1 minute; Run for 23 minutes = 34 minutes

DAY 3 Run for 10 minutes; Walk for 1 minute; Run for 25 minutes = 36 minutes

WEEK 8

DAY 1 Run for 26 minutes = 26 minutes
DAY 2 Run for 28 minutes = 28 minutes
DAY 3 Run for 30 minutes = 30 minutes

WEEK 9

Start! Your First 5K

Summary

...still on getting set? Here is a brief recap of the details:

The journey to becoming a runner is similar to that of becoming successful in life. The rules are almost the same; it all starts from convincing yourself, because no one can do it for you; there are limits, but they are only to be broken; there would be distractions, you have to keep going; when you get to the finishing line, take a brief rest, and take up another race, because you can't afford to stay in one place and not keep going.

Becoming fit and having a physical shape has healthy and emotional benefits. If you will enjoy these benefits, then you must avoid some common mistakes most beginners make.

Live like a runner, take your schedule serious, watch what you consume, keep yourself motivated, get the needed apps, then, go all out training, using the schedule that works better for you. Whatever schedule you pick, you can be sure you will be set to run in the seventh week.

What are you waiting for?

You now know everything a beginner needs to know, but you don't have to stop there. You have to continue so you can leave the beginner's level.

Set goals and records and break them. Stay in form. Extend it to a 10K run. Upgrade your level. And the most important thing: always dare to beat your life record, because you can. **YES, YOU CAN!**

You are good to go! Go for your first 5K and see how amazing you are going to perform.

SUMMARY

On Your Mark! Get Set!! Go!!!

Answers to Common Questions

Where is the right place to run?

Look for routes on your local roads that have minimal traffic. When running on them, never forget to follow the safety precautions like running in the opposite direction of traffic so that you can see whatever is coming your way clearly. Running on the same road can soon get boring. Try moving to a different road because it will help your body and mind. Route finder apps will help you discover some routes around your area, or you can search "best places to run near me," and get some great ideas. You can also try a real track by going to a nearby high school. Away from home, speak to hotel staff or try locating a school as well. Just don't do it on the same route for long.

Can I take walk intervals during runs?

Many runners have associated walking during runs to being lazy and too weak to go, but it is not so. It actually gives the muscles a chance to rest and recover, and lowers your heart rate. Don't wait until you are too tired to go. When you notice you are getting tired and you don't want to stop, you can lower the speed gradually until you start walking. However, don't take it as a chance to slow down completely. Keep your elbows at a 90-degree angle and not your side and take quick steps.

Is it right to keep running while in pain?

Sometimes, you may feel pain in your muscles. It is because they have not recovered completely. While this may not stop you from going, make sure you don't go too hard, or too fast. If you feel pain in particular parts of the body, then take caution so you don't overdo it. Follow the tips in this guide to ensure you have a positive experience. For example, being dehydrated may lead to headaches, and running with a bad posture my lead to neck pain. Take the pain level (0-10) into account. Less than 4, go softly. If it gets to 5, you must refrain from running to recover, or go for recovery cross-trainings.

When will running become easy for me?

You have started running and you think in a matter of two weeks, it is going to get easy for you. Well, it might, but the way a person's body adapts is different. Some people, after hitting the 30 minute run, find the rest easy, and some will have to wait for weeks. If it is taking too much time, just keep doing it. Don't be too insistent on fast paced or going far. Take it as it comes, and soon your body will adapt. However, running does not ever get so easy that you don't know you are doing something. No! It gets a little easy, you make up for the rest with your motivation. Read the tips on how to stay motivated.

How do I get rid of side stitches?

Although the real cause of side stitches is not so clear, there are simple cautions to take to reduce the chances. Don't go to run too soon after eating. Starting a run after eating when you are still full could lead to side stitches. Avoid sweet beverages as much as you can. Don't just jump into a run without warming up, and always cool down after running. Don't breathe in a shallow way. Breathe at the stomach level and assist your nose with your mouth. You can read about breathing tips in this guide.

Thank you

First of all, thank you for reading my book. I know you could have picked any number of books to read, but you picked this book and for that I am extremely grateful.

If you enjoyed my book and found some benefit in reading this, I'd like to hear from you and hope that you could take some time to post a review on Amazon. Your feedback and support will help me to greatly improve my writing craft for future projects and make this book even better.

I want you, the reader, to know that your review is very important and so, if you'd like to leave a review.

I wish you all the best in your first 5K Run!

About the Author

"We all deserve to live a happy and well-balanced life! It is not a secret recipe given to just a few. It is a lifetime gift available for everyone who really wants it."

Tomasz's mission and source of personal satisfaction is helping people by sharing his knowledge and experience with everyone who wants to live a happy, well-balanced life, concentrating on core values, self-esteem, beloved family, and a great job.

Tomasz is a content man enjoying a calm and happy family life, with growing children. He loves spending time with family and learning how to enjoy the small things in life.

He lives a healthy and sporty life caring about good mental and physical condition, balanced diet, and regular exercise. Every year, Tomasz beats his own record for a 10K run; the last one stands at 47 minutes 13 seconds. This year the challenge is to run below 46 minutes. Keep your fingers crossed!

Tomasz manages to work full-time for a multinational company and has developed new projects on his own. He is a marketing enthusiast with 17 year's experience and has achieved success as a marketer and team manager.

His previous perspective was not so optimistic. He struggled with everyday issues, i.e., paying off a high mortgage, an overwhelming job, raising children, and lack of time for himself. Additional worries created health issues, chronic stress, and a general feeling of decreasing physical condition.

He knew he had to change his life. So, Tomasz changed his perspective; stopped worrying and started to actively forge his life, one step at a time.

You can connect with me on:

🌐 https://yourlifehabits.com

Subscribe to my newsletter:

✉ https://yourlifehabits.com/newsletter

Also by Tomasz Tomaszewski

7 Effective Skills to Boost Your Life Energy - FREE eBOOK

Are you overwhelmed, stressed, and feel that everything is going too fast?

If you want to change your state of mind, boost your life energy, and introduce happiness to your life, this book is for you.

You will be given a set of practical exercises that you can try out immediately. Ten to fifteen minutes a day makes a real difference. **In three to four weeks you will benefit much more than you think.**

Are you ready to boost your life energy?

Printed in Great Britain
by Amazon